_____
INSERT NAME

IS NOT DEFINED BY THE ENDING OF THIS RELATIONSHIP. IN FACT, I AM INSPIRED, EMPOWERED AND ENERGIZED.

FLIGHTS IN *Stilettos*

Beloved,

Fantasia Barrino said it best in her song "I'm Doing Me" she says:

> If you can't love me equally,
> Then you don't need to be with me
> Nothing more beautiful then knowing you're worth
> And finally, yeah uh
> I know exactly what I deserve
>
> Doin' me, this time around
> Doin' me, don't need you now.

Yes, breakups hurt, and they are an inevitable part of human connections. However, relationships are beautiful experiences when people are equally yoked and divinely meant for each other.

Then there are times when you have to experience sifting through the weeds before that rose that's meant just for you emerges and sweeps you off of your feet.

But that's not what this diary is about. This diary is about you loving yourself despite the broken relationship, and despite the messages and thoughts replaying in your mind about how you have failed, and that you're unworthy, that you'll never love again, and that you've lost the best thing you ever had. Those are all lies. There's no reason to believe any of that. You will experience romance and reciprocated love again.

However, it is essential to recognize when your emotions are consumed with thoughts about your ex and if you're experiencing an emotional crisis resulting from your relationship ending. If this is your situation, seek the help of a mental health provider immediately.

Trust that you are worthy, you are loved, you are valued, you are exquisite, you are unique, you have a sense of humor, you have a purpose, you are destined for greatness, you will love again, and you will emerge wiser and better equipped to deal with the next set of challenges that will come your way.

You've got this!

This journal will give you the inspiration, motivation, and determination to "do you" and to put yourself first and move forward.

Breathe, sis; it will be okay.

Xo,

Kinyatta

20 WAYS
TO MAKE YOURSELF A PRIORITY

1. Practice being grateful for your existence
2. Practice mindfulness
3. Practice meditation daily
4. Practice being thankful for your resources, career and supportive friends
5. Visualize being happy and peaceful
6. Burn your favorite scented candles
7. Burn sage
8. Practice journaling your feelings, thoughts and emotions
9. Buy one splurge item
10. Connect with supportive friends
11. Enjoy a relaxing spa day
12. Enjoy an exquisite meal at a new restaurant
13. Take a dream vacation/solo trip or girls trip
14. Change your hairstyle
15. Consult with a fashion stylist and add a few new pieces to your wardrobe
16. Crack open your favorite expensive wine or champagne and listen to your favorite "girl power" songs
17. Read books about self-healing and self-empowerment
18. Consult with a makeup artist and create a new look and change your lipstick color
19. Spend time with people that you consider wise, trustworthy, loving and sincere. Learn from them.
20. Look in the mirror everyday and tell yourself with certainty that you are worthy and that this too shall pass.

7-DAYS
OF SELF-LOVE QUOTES

SUNDAY
"You carry so much love in your heart. Give some to yourself."
~ R.Z.

MONDAY
"No one is you and that is your superpower." ~UNKNOWN

TUESDAY
"She remembered who she was and changed the game."
~Lalah Deliah

WEDNESDAY
"In order to love who you are, you cannot hate the experiences that shaped you." ~ Andrea Dykstra

THURSDAY
"I inhale positive energy and exhale any fears." ~UNKNOWN

FRIDAY
"My imperfections make me beautiful." ~ Suzanne Heyn

SATURDAY
"Your greatest responsibility is to love yourself and to know that you are enough." ~UNKNOWN

I'M DOING ME...VENTING LOG

It's perfectly okay to vent to express your disappointment and your frustrations.
Let your ex "have it" right here and only here because, Queen, you're focusing on yourself!

_____

_____

_____

_____

_____

_____

_____

_____

_____

_____

_____

_____

_____

_____

_____

_____

_____

_____

I'M DOING ME...VENTING LOG

_____

_____

_____

_____

_____

_____

_____

_____

_____

_____

_____

_____

_____

_____

_____

_____

_____

_____

_____

_____

I'M DOING ME...VENTING LOG

I'M DOING ME...VENTING LOG

I'M DOING ME...VENTING LOG

_____

_____

_____

_____

_____

_____

_____

_____

_____

_____

_____

_____

_____

_____

_____

_____

_____

_____

_____

_____

_____

_____

_____

I'M DOING ME...SELF-REFLECTIONS

Date: /   /

	Today I Feel:
I thought about my ex today and I:	☐ Stressed
	☐ Tearful
I made myself a priority today by:	☐ Angry
	☐ Sad
	☐ Lonely
	☐ In need of answers
I didn't think about my breakup when I:	☐ Fearful
	☐ Peaceful
	☐ Acceptance
	☐ Forgiveness

The biggest challenge I faced today was:

I experienced a "boss up" moment today when I:

I felt at peace today when I:

I loved myself today when I:

I am: (List three positive attributes about yourself)

1.

2.

3.

I am working to improve myself in these areas:

I'M DOING ME...SELF-REFLECTIONS

Date: /   /

I thought about my ex today and I:	**Today I Feel:**
	☐ Stressed
	☐ Tearful
I made myself a priority today by:	☐ Angry
	☐ Sad
	☐ Lonely
	☐ In need of answers
I didn't think about my breakup when I:	☐ Fearful
	☐ Peaceful
	☐ Acceptance
	☐ Forgiveness

The biggest challenge I faced today was:

I experienced a "boss up" moment today when I:

I felt at peace today when I:

I loved myself today when I:

I am: (List three positive attributes about yourself)

1.

2.

3.

I am working to improve myself in these areas:

I'M DOING ME...SELF-REFLECTIONS

Date: /   /

	Today I Feel:
I thought about my ex today and I:	☐ Stressed
	☐ Tearful
I made myself a priority today by:	☐ Angry
	☐ Sad
	☐ Lonely
	☐ In need of answers
I didn't think about my breakup when I:	☐ Fearful
	☐ Peaceful
	☐ Acceptance
	☐ Forgiveness

The biggest challenge I faced today was:

I experienced a "boss up" moment today when I:

I felt at peace today when I:

I loved myself today when I:

I am: (List three positive attributes about yourself)

1.

2.

3.

I am working to improve myself in these areas:

I'M DOING ME...SELF-REFLECTIONS

Date: / /

I thought about my ex today and I:	**Today I Feel:**
	☐ Stressed
	☐ Tearful
I made myself a priority today by:	☐ Angry
	☐ Sad
	☐ Lonely
	☐ In need of answers
I didn't think about my breakup when I:	☐ Fearful
	☐ Peaceful
	☐ Acceptance
	☐ Forgiveness

The biggest challenge I faced today was:

I experienced a "boss up" moment today when I:

I felt at peace today when I:

I loved myself today when I:

I am: (List three positive attributes about yourself)

1.

2.

3.

I am working to improve myself in these areas:

I'M DOING ME...SELF-REFLECTIONS

Date: /   /

I thought about my ex today and I:	Today I Feel:
	☐ Stressed
	☐ Tearful
I made myself a priority today by:	☐ Angry
	☐ Sad
	☐ Lonely
	☐ In need of answers
I didn't think about my breakup when I:	☐ Fearful
	☐ Peaceful
	☐ Acceptance
	☐ Forgiveness

The biggest challenge I faced today was:

I experienced a "boss up" moment today when I:

I felt at peace today when I:

I loved myself today when I:

I am: (List three positive attributes about yourself)

1.

2.

3.

I am working to improve myself in these areas:

I'M DOING ME...SELF-REFLECTIONS

Date: /   /

I thought about my ex today and I:	**Today I Feel:**
	☐ Stressed
	☐ Tearful
I made myself a priority today by:	☐ Angry
	☐ Sad
	☐ Lonely
	☐ In need of answers
I didn't think about my breakup when I:	☐ Fearful
	☐ Peaceful
	☐ Acceptance
	☐ Forgiveness

The biggest challenge I faced today was:

I experienced a "boss up" moment today when I:

I felt at peace today when I:

I loved myself today when I:

I am: (List three positive attributes about yourself)

1.

2.

3.

I am working to improve myself in these areas:

I'M DOING ME...SELF-REFLECTIONS

Date: /   /

I thought about my ex today and I:	Today I Feel:
	☐ Stressed
	☐ Tearful
I made myself a priority today by:	☐ Angry
	☐ Sad
	☐ Lonely
	☐ In need of answers
I didn't think about my breakup when I:	☐ Fearful
	☐ Peaceful
	☐ Acceptance
	☐ Forgiveness

The biggest challenge I faced today was:

I experienced a "boss up" moment today when I:

I felt at peace today when I:

I loved myself today when I:

I am: (List three positive attributes about yourself)

1.

2.

3.

I am working to improve myself in these areas:

I'M DOING ME...SELF-REFLECTIONS

Date: /   /

I thought about my ex today and I:	**Today I Feel:**
	☐ Stressed
	☐ Tearful
I made myself a priority today by:	☐ Angry
	☐ Sad
	☐ Lonely
	☐ In need of answers
I didn't think about my breakup when I:	☐ Fearful
	☐ Peaceful
	☐ Acceptance
	☐ Forgiveness

The biggest challenge I faced today was:

I experienced a "boss up" moment today when I:

I felt at peace today when I:

I loved myself today when I:

I am: (List three positive attributes about yourself)

1.

2.

3.

I am working to improve myself in these areas:

I'M DOING ME...SELF-REFLECTIONS

Date: /   /

	Today I Feel:
I thought about my ex today and I:	☐ Stressed
	☐ Tearful
I made myself a priority today by:	☐ Angry
	☐ Sad
	☐ Lonely
	☐ In need of answers
I didn't think about my breakup when I:	☐ Fearful
	☐ Peaceful
	☐ Acceptance
	☐ Forgiveness

The biggest challenge I faced today was:

I experienced a "boss up" moment today when I:

I felt at peace today when I:

I loved myself today when I:

I am: (List three positive attributes about yourself)

1.

2.

3.

I am working to improve myself in these areas:

I'M DOING ME...SELF-REFLECTIONS

Date: /   /

I thought about my ex today and I:	**Today I Feel:**
	☐ Stressed
	☐ Tearful
I made myself a priority today by:	☐ Angry
	☐ Sad
	☐ Lonely
	☐ In need of answers
I didn't think about my breakup when I:	☐ Fearful
	☐ Peaceful
	☐ Acceptance
	☐ Forgiveness

The biggest challenge I faced today was:

I experienced a "boss up" moment today when I:

I felt at peace today when I:

I loved myself today when I:

I am: (List three positive attributes about yourself)

1.

2.

3.

I am working to improve myself in these areas:

I'M DOING ME...SELF-REFLECTIONS

Date: / /

I thought about my ex today and I:	**Today I Feel:** ☐ Stressed ☐ Tearful ☐ Angry ☐ Sad ☐ Lonely ☐ In need of answers ☐ Fearful ☐ Peaceful ☐ Acceptance ☐ Forgiveness
I made myself a priority today by:	
I didn't think about my breakup when I:	

The biggest challenge I faced today was:

I experienced a "boss up" moment today when I:

I felt at peace today when I:

I loved myself today when I:

I am: (List three positive attributes about yourself)

1.

2.

3.

I am working to improve myself in these areas:

I'M DOING ME...SELF-REFLECTIONS

Date: /   /

I thought about my ex today and I:	**Today I Feel:**
	☐ Stressed
	☐ Tearful
I made myself a priority today by:	☐ Angry
	☐ Sad
	☐ Lonely
	☐ In need of answers
I didn't think about my breakup when I:	☐ Fearful
	☐ Peaceful
	☐ Acceptance
	☐ Forgiveness

The biggest challenge I faced today was:

I experienced a "boss up" moment today when I:

I felt at peace today when I:

I loved myself today when I:

I am: (List three positive attributes about yourself)

1.

2.

3.

I am working to improve myself in these areas:

I'M DOING ME...SELF-REFLECTIONS

Date: /   /

I thought about my ex today and I:	**Today I Feel:**
	☐ Stressed
	☐ Tearful
I made myself a priority today by:	☐ Angry
	☐ Sad
	☐ Lonely
	☐ In need of answers
I didn't think about my breakup when I:	☐ Fearful
	☐ Peaceful
	☐ Acceptance
	☐ Forgiveness

The biggest challenge I faced today was:

I experienced a "boss up" moment today when I:

I felt at peace today when I:

I loved myself today when I:

I am: (List three positive attributes about yourself)

1.

2.

3.

I am working to improve myself in these areas:

I'M DOING ME...SELF-REFLECTIONS

Date: /   /

I thought about my ex today and I:	**Today I Feel:**
	☐ Stressed
	☐ Tearful
I made myself a priority today by:	☐ Angry
	☐ Sad
	☐ Lonely
	☐ In need of answers
I didn't think about my breakup when I:	☐ Fearful
	☐ Peaceful
	☐ Acceptance
	☐ Forgiveness

The biggest challenge I faced today was:

I experienced a "boss up" moment today when I:

I felt at peace today when I:

I loved myself today when I:

I am: (List three positive attributes about yourself)

1.

2.

3.

I am working to improve myself in these areas:

I'M DOING ME...SELF-REFLECTIONS

Date: /   /

I thought about my ex today and I:	**Today I Feel:** ☐ Stressed ☐ Tearful
I made myself a priority today by:	☐ Angry ☐ Sad ☐ Lonely ☐ In need of answers
I didn't think about my breakup when I:	☐ Fearful ☐ Peaceful ☐ Acceptance ☐ Forgiveness

The biggest challenge I faced today was:

I experienced a "boss up" moment today when I:

I felt at peace today when I:

I loved myself today when I:

I am: (List three positive attributes about yourself)

1.

2.

3.

I am working to improve myself in these areas:

I'M DOING ME...SELF-REFLECTIONS

Date: ___ / ___ / ___

I thought about my ex today and I:	**Today I Feel:** ☐ Stressed ☐ Tearful
I made myself a priority today by:	☐ Angry ☐ Sad ☐ Lonely ☐ In need of answers
I didn't think about my breakup when I:	☐ Fearful ☐ Peaceful ☐ Acceptance ☐ Forgiveness

The biggest challenge I faced today was:

I experienced a "boss up" moment today when I:

I felt at peace today when I:

I loved myself today when I:

I am: (List three positive attributes about yourself)

1.

2.

3.

I am working to improve myself in these areas:

I'M DOING ME...SELF-REFLECTIONS

Date: /   /

	Today I Feel:
I thought about my ex today and I:	☐ Stressed
	☐ Tearful
I made myself a priority today by:	☐ Angry
	☐ Sad
	☐ Lonely
	☐ In need of answers
I didn't think about my breakup when I:	☐ Fearful
	☐ Peaceful
	☐ Acceptance
	☐ Forgiveness

The biggest challenge I faced today was:

I experienced a "boss up" moment today when I:

I felt at peace today when I:

I loved myself today when I:

I am: (List three positive attributes about yourself)

1.

2.

3.

I am working to improve myself in these areas:

I'M DOING ME...SELF-REFLECTIONS

Date: /   /

	Today I Feel:
I thought about my ex today and I:	☐ Stressed ☐ Tearful
I made myself a priority today by:	☐ Angry ☐ Sad ☐ Lonely ☐ In need of answers
I didn't think about my breakup when I:	☐ Fearful ☐ Peaceful ☐ Acceptance ☐ Forgiveness

The biggest challenge I faced today was:

I experienced a "boss up" moment today when I:

I felt at peace today when I:

I loved myself today when I:

I am: (List three positive attributes about yourself)

1.

2.

3.

I am working to improve myself in these areas:

I'M DOING ME...SELF-REFLECTIONS

Date: /   /

I thought about my ex today and I:	**Today I Feel:**
	☐ Stressed
	☐ Tearful
I made myself a priority today by:	☐ Angry
	☐ Sad
	☐ Lonely
	☐ In need of answers
I didn't think about my breakup when I:	☐ Fearful
	☐ Peaceful
	☐ Acceptance
	☐ Forgiveness

The biggest challenge I faced today was:

I experienced a "boss up" moment today when I:

I felt at peace today when I:

I loved myself today when I:

I am: (List three positive attributes about yourself)

1.

2.

3.

I am working to improve myself in these areas:

I'M DOING ME...SELF-REFLECTIONS

Date: /   /

I thought about my ex today and I:	**Today I Feel:**
	☐ Stressed
	☐ Tearful
I made myself a priority today by:	☐ Angry
	☐ Sad
	☐ Lonely
	☐ In need of answers
I didn't think about my breakup when I:	☐ Fearful
	☐ Peaceful
	☐ Acceptance
	☐ Forgiveness

The biggest challenge I faced today was:

I experienced a "boss up" moment today when I:

I felt at peace today when I:

I loved myself today when I:

I am: (List three positive attributes about yourself)

1.

2.

3.

I am working to improve myself in these areas:

I'M DOING ME...SELF-REFLECTIONS

Date: /   /

I thought about my ex today and I:	**Today I Feel:**
	☐ Stressed
	☐ Tearful
I made myself a priority today by:	☐ Angry
	☐ Sad
	☐ Lonely
	☐ In need of answers
I didn't think about my breakup when I:	☐ Fearful
	☐ Peaceful
	☐ Acceptance
	☐ Forgiveness

The biggest challenge I faced today was:

I experienced a "boss up" moment today when I:

I felt at peace today when I:

I loved myself today when I:

I am: (List three positive attributes about yourself)

1.

2.

3.

I am working to improve myself in these areas:

I'M DOING ME...SELF-REFLECTIONS

Date: /   /

	Today I Feel:
I thought about my ex today and I:	☐ Stressed
	☐ Tearful
I made myself a priority today by:	☐ Angry
	☐ Sad
	☐ Lonely
	☐ In need of answers
I didn't think about my breakup when I:	☐ Fearful
	☐ Peaceful
	☐ Acceptance
	☐ Forgiveness

The biggest challenge I faced today was:

I experienced a "boss up" moment today when I:

I felt at peace today when I:

I loved myself today when I:

I am: (List three positive attributes about yourself)

1.

2.

3.

I am working to improve myself in these areas:

I'M DOING ME...SELF-REFLECTIONS

Date: /   /

I thought about my ex today and I:	**Today I Feel:**
	☐ Stressed
	☐ Tearful
I made myself a priority today by:	☐ Angry
	☐ Sad
	☐ Lonely
	☐ In need of answers
I didn't think about my breakup when I:	☐ Fearful
	☐ Peaceful
	☐ Acceptance
	☐ Forgiveness

The biggest challenge I faced today was:

I experienced a "boss up" moment today when I:

I felt at peace today when I:

I loved myself today when I:

I am: (List three positive attributes about yourself)

1.

2.

3.

I am working to improve myself in these areas:

I'M DOING ME...SELF-REFLECTIONS

Date: ____ / ____ / ____

	Today I Feel:
I thought about my ex today and I:	☐ Stressed
	☐ Tearful
I made myself a priority today by:	☐ Angry
	☐ Sad
	☐ Lonely
	☐ In need of answers
I didn't think about my breakup when I:	☐ Fearful
	☐ Peaceful
	☐ Acceptance
	☐ Forgiveness

The biggest challenge I faced today was:

I experienced a "boss up" moment today when I:

I felt at peace today when I:

I loved myself today when I:

I am: (List three positive attributes about yourself)

1.

2.

3.

I am working to improve myself in these areas:

I'M DOING ME...SELF-REFLECTIONS

Date: /   /

I thought about my ex today and I:	**Today I Feel:**
	☐ Stressed
	☐ Tearful
I made myself a priority today by:	☐ Angry
	☐ Sad
	☐ Lonely
	☐ In need of answers
I didn't think about my breakup when I:	☐ Fearful
	☐ Peaceful
	☐ Acceptance
	☐ Forgiveness

The biggest challenge I faced today was:

I experienced a "boss up" moment today when I:

I felt at peace today when I:

I loved myself today when I:

I am: (List three positive attributes about yourself)

1.

2.

3.

I am working to improve myself in these areas:

I'M DOING ME...SELF-REFLECTIONS

Date: /   /

I thought about my ex today and I:	**Today I Feel:** ☐ Stressed ☐ Tearful
I made myself a priority today by:	☐ Angry ☐ Sad ☐ Lonely ☐ In need of answers
I didn't think about my breakup when I:	☐ Fearful ☐ Peaceful ☐ Acceptance ☐ Forgiveness

The biggest challenge I faced today was:

I experienced a "boss up" moment today when I:

I felt at peace today when I:

I loved myself today when I:

I am: (List three positive attributes about yourself)

1.

2.

3.

I am working to improve myself in these areas:

I'M DOING ME...SELF-REFLECTIONS

Date: /   /

I thought about my ex today and I:	**Today I Feel:**
	☐ Stressed
	☐ Tearful
I made myself a priority today by:	☐ Angry
	☐ Sad
	☐ Lonely
	☐ In need of answers
I didn't think about my breakup when I:	☐ Fearful
	☐ Peaceful
	☐ Acceptance
	☐ Forgiveness

The biggest challenge I faced today was:

I experienced a "boss up" moment today when I:

I felt at peace today when I:

I loved myself today when I:

I am: (List three positive attributes about yourself)

1.

2.

3.

I am working to improve myself in these areas:

I'M DOING ME...SELF-REFLECTIONS

Date: ___ / ___ / ___

I thought about my ex today and I:	Today I Feel:
	☐ Stressed
	☐ Tearful
I made myself a priority today by:	☐ Angry
	☐ Sad
	☐ Lonely
	☐ In need of answers
I didn't think about my breakup when I:	☐ Fearful
	☐ Peaceful
	☐ Acceptance
	☐ Forgiveness

The biggest challenge I faced today was:

I experienced a "boss up" moment today when I:

I felt at peace today when I:

I loved myself today when I:

I am: (List three positive attributes about yourself)

1.

2.

3.

I am working to improve myself in these areas:

I'M DOING ME...SELF-REFLECTIONS

Date: /   /

	Today I Feel:
I thought about my ex today and I:	☐ Stressed
	☐ Tearful
I made myself a priority today by:	☐ Angry
	☐ Sad
	☐ Lonely
	☐ In need of answers
I didn't think about my breakup when I:	☐ Fearful
	☐ Peaceful
	☐ Acceptance
	☐ Forgiveness

The biggest challenge I faced today was:

I experienced a "boss up" moment today when I:

I felt at peace today when I:

I loved myself today when I:

I am: (List three positive attributes about yourself)

1.

2.

3.

I am working to improve myself in these areas:

I'M DOING ME...SELF-REFLECTIONS

Date: /   /

I thought about my ex today and I:	**Today I Feel:** ☐ Stressed ☐ Tearful
I made myself a priority today by:	☐ Angry ☐ Sad ☐ Lonely ☐ In need of answers
I didn't think about my breakup when I:	☐ Fearful ☐ Peaceful ☐ Acceptance ☐ Forgiveness

The biggest challenge I faced today was:

I experienced a "boss up" moment today when I:

I felt at peace today when I:

I loved myself today when I:

I am: (List three positive attributes about yourself)

1.

2.

3.

I am working to improve myself in these areas:

I'M DOING ME...SELF-REFLECTIONS

Date: / /

	Today I Feel:
I thought about my ex today and I:	☐ Stressed
	☐ Tearful
I made myself a priority today by:	☐ Angry
	☐ Sad
	☐ Lonely
	☐ In need of answers
I didn't think about my breakup when I:	☐ Fearful
	☐ Peaceful
	☐ Acceptance
	☐ Forgiveness

The biggest challenge I faced today was:

I experienced a "boss up" moment today when I:

I felt at peace today when I:

I loved myself today when I:

I am: (List three positive attributes about yourself)

1.

2.

3.

I am working to improve myself in these areas:

I'M DOING ME...SELF-REFLECTIONS

Date: /   /

I thought about my ex today and I:	**Today I Feel:** ☐ Stressed ☐ Tearful
I made myself a priority today by:	☐ Angry ☐ Sad ☐ Lonely ☐ In need of answers
I didn't think about my breakup when I:	☐ Fearful ☐ Peaceful ☐ Acceptance ☐ Forgiveness

The biggest challenge I faced today was:

I experienced a "boss up" moment today when I:

I felt at peace today when I:

I loved myself today when I:

I am: (List three positive attributes about yourself)

1.

2.

3.

I am working to improve myself in these areas:

I'M DOING ME...SELF-REFLECTIONS

Date: /   /

I thought about my ex today and I:	**Today I Feel:** ☐ Stressed ☐ Tearful
I made myself a priority today by:	☐ Angry ☐ Sad ☐ Lonely ☐ In need of answers
I didn't think about my breakup when I:	☐ Fearful ☐ Peaceful ☐ Acceptance ☐ Forgiveness

The biggest challenge I faced today was:

I experienced a "boss up" moment today when I:

I felt at peace today when I:

I loved myself today when I:

I am: (List three positive attributes about yourself)

1.

2.

3.

I am working to improve myself in these areas:

I'M DOING ME...SELF-REFLECTIONS

Date: /   /

I thought about my ex today and I:	**Today I Feel:** ☐ Stressed ☐ Tearful
I made myself a priority today by:	☐ Angry ☐ Sad ☐ Lonely ☐ In need of answers
I didn't think about my breakup when I:	☐ Fearful ☐ Peaceful ☐ Acceptance ☐ Forgiveness

The biggest challenge I faced today was:

I experienced a "boss up" moment today when I:

I felt at peace today when I:

I loved myself today when I:

I am: (List three positive attributes about yourself)

1.

2.

3.

I am working to improve myself in these areas:

I'M DOING ME...SELF-REFLECTIONS

Date: / /

I thought about my ex today and I:	**Today I Feel:**
	☐ Stressed
	☐ Tearful
I made myself a priority today by:	☐ Angry
	☐ Sad
	☐ Lonely
	☐ In need of answers
I didn't think about my breakup when I:	☐ Fearful
	☐ Peaceful
	☐ Acceptance
	☐ Forgiveness

The biggest challenge I faced today was:

I experienced a "boss up" moment today when I:

I felt at peace today when I:

I loved myself today when I:

I am: (List three positive attributes about yourself)

1.

2.

3.

I am working to improve myself in these areas:

I'M DOING ME...SELF-REFLECTIONS

Date: /   /

I thought about my ex today and I:	**Today I Feel:**
	☐ Stressed
	☐ Tearful
I made myself a priority today by:	☐ Angry
	☐ Sad
	☐ Lonely
	☐ In need of answers
I didn't think about my breakup when I:	☐ Fearful
	☐ Peaceful
	☐ Acceptance
	☐ Forgiveness

The biggest challenge I faced today was:

I experienced a "boss up" moment today when I:

I felt at peace today when I:

I loved myself today when I:

I am: (List three positive attributes about yourself)

1.

2.

3.

I am working to improve myself in these areas:

I'M DOING ME...SELF-REFLECTIONS

Date: /   /

I thought about my ex today and I:	**Today I Feel:**
	☐ Stressed
	☐ Tearful
I made myself a priority today by:	☐ Angry
	☐ Sad
	☐ Lonely
	☐ In need of answers
I didn't think about my breakup when I:	☐ Fearful
	☐ Peaceful
	☐ Acceptance
	☐ Forgiveness

The biggest challenge I faced today was:

I experienced a "boss up" moment today when I:

I felt at peace today when I:

I loved myself today when I:

I am: (List three positive attributes about yourself)

1.

2.

3.

I am working to improve myself in these areas:

I'M DOING ME...SELF-REFLECTIONS

Date: /   /

I thought about my ex today and I:	**Today I Feel:**
	☐ Stressed
	☐ Tearful
I made myself a priority today by:	☐ Angry
	☐ Sad
	☐ Lonely
	☐ In need of answers
I didn't think about my breakup when I:	☐ Fearful
	☐ Peaceful
	☐ Acceptance
	☐ Forgiveness

The biggest challenge I faced today was:

I experienced a "boss up" moment today when I:

I felt at peace today when I:

I loved myself today when I:

I am: (List three positive attributes about yourself)

1.

2.

3.

I am working to improve myself in these areas:

I'M DOING ME...SELF-REFLECTIONS

Date: /   /

I thought about my ex today and I:	**Today I Feel:** ☐ Stressed ☐ Tearful
I made myself a priority today by:	☐ Angry ☐ Sad ☐ Lonely
	☐ In need of answers
I didn't think about my breakup when I:	☐ Fearful ☐ Peaceful ☐ Acceptance ☐ Forgiveness

The biggest challenge I faced today was:

I experienced a "boss up" moment today when I:

I felt at peace today when I:

I loved myself today when I:

I am: (List three positive attributes about yourself)

1.

2.

3.

I am working to improve myself in these areas:

I'M DOING ME...SELF-REFLECTIONS

Date: /   /

I thought about my ex today and I:	**Today I Feel:** ☐ Stressed ☐ Tearful
I made myself a priority today by:	☐ Angry ☐ Sad ☐ Lonely ☐ In need of answers
I didn't think about my breakup when I:	☐ Fearful ☐ Peaceful ☐ Acceptance ☐ Forgiveness

The biggest challenge I faced today was:

I experienced a "boss up" moment today when I:

I felt at peace today when I:

I loved myself today when I:

I am: (List three positive attributes about yourself)

1.

2.

3.

I am working to improve myself in these areas:

I'M DOING ME...SELF-REFLECTIONS

Date: /   /

	Today I Feel:
I thought about my ex today and I:	☐ Stressed
	☐ Tearful
	☐ Angry
I made myself a priority today by:	☐ Sad
	☐ Lonely
	☐ In need of answers
I didn't think about my breakup when I:	☐ Fearful
	☐ Peaceful
	☐ Acceptance
	☐ Forgiveness

The biggest challenge I faced today was:

I experienced a "boss up" moment today when I:

I felt at peace today when I:

I loved myself today when I:

I am: (List three positive attributes about yourself)

1.

2.

3.

I am working to improve myself in these areas:

I'M DOING ME...SELF-REFLECTIONS

Date: /   /

I thought about my ex today and I:	**Today I Feel:** ☐ Stressed ☐ Tearful
I made myself a priority today by:	☐ Angry ☐ Sad ☐ Lonely ☐ In need of answers
I didn't think about my breakup when I:	☐ Fearful ☐ Peaceful ☐ Acceptance ☐ Forgiveness

The biggest challenge I faced today was:

I experienced a "boss up" moment today when I:

I felt at peace today when I:

I loved myself today when I:

I am: (List three positive attributes about yourself)

1.

2.

3.

I am working to improve myself in these areas:

I'M DOING ME...SELF-REFLECTIONS

Date: /   /

I thought about my ex today and I:	**Today I Feel:** ☐ Stressed ☐ Tearful ☐ Angry ☐ Sad ☐ Lonely ☐ In need of answers ☐ Fearful ☐ Peaceful ☐ Acceptance ☐ Forgiveness
I made myself a priority today by:	
I didn't think about my breakup when I:	

The biggest challenge I faced today was:

I experienced a "boss up" moment today when I:

I felt at peace today when I:

I loved myself today when I:

I am: (List three positive attributes about yourself)

1.

2.

3.

I am working to improve myself in these areas:

I'M DOING ME...SELF-REFLECTIONS

Date: / /

I thought about my ex today and I:	**Today I Feel:**
	☐ Stressed
	☐ Tearful
I made myself a priority today by:	☐ Angry
	☐ Sad
	☐ Lonely
	☐ In need of answers
I didn't think about my breakup when I:	☐ Fearful
	☐ Peaceful
	☐ Acceptance
	☐ Forgiveness

The biggest challenge I faced today was:

I experienced a "boss up" moment today when I:

I felt at peace today when I:

I loved myself today when I:

I am: (List three positive attributes about yourself)

1.

2.

3.

I am working to improve myself in these areas:

I'M DOING ME...SELF-REFLECTIONS

Date: /   /

	Today I Feel:
I thought about my ex today and I:	☐ Stressed
	☐ Tearful
I made myself a priority today by:	☐ Angry
	☐ Sad
	☐ Lonely
	☐ In need of answers
I didn't think about my breakup when I:	☐ Fearful
	☐ Peaceful
	☐ Acceptance
	☐ Forgiveness

The biggest challenge I faced today was:

I experienced a "boss up" moment today when I:

I felt at peace today when I:

I loved myself today when I:

I am: (List three positive attributes about yourself)

1.

2.

3.

I am working to improve myself in these areas:

I'M DOING ME...SELF-REFLECTIONS

Date: /   /

	Today I Feel:
I thought about my ex today and I:	☐ Stressed ☐ Tearful
I made myself a priority today by:	☐ Angry ☐ Sad ☐ Lonely ☐ In need of answers
I didn't think about my breakup when I:	☐ Fearful ☐ Peaceful ☐ Acceptance ☐ Forgiveness

The biggest challenge I faced today was:

I experienced a "boss up" moment today when I:

I felt at peace today when I:

I loved myself today when I:

I am: (List three positive attributes about yourself)

1.

2.

3.

I am working to improve myself in these areas:

I'M DOING ME...SELF-REFLECTIONS

Date: /   /

	Today I Feel:
I thought about my ex today and I:	☐ Stressed
	☐ Tearful
I made myself a priority today by:	☐ Angry
	☐ Sad
	☐ Lonely
	☐ In need of answers
I didn't think about my breakup when I:	☐ Fearful
	☐ Peaceful
	☐ Acceptance
	☐ Forgiveness

The biggest challenge I faced today was:

I experienced a "boss up" moment today when I:

I felt at peace today when I:

I loved myself today when I:

I am: (List three positive attributes about yourself)

1.

2.

3.

I am working to improve myself in these areas:

I'M DOING ME...SELF-REFLECTIONS

Date: /   /

I thought about my ex today and I:	Today I Feel:
	☐ Stressed
	☐ Tearful
I made myself a priority today by:	☐ Angry
	☐ Sad
	☐ Lonely
	☐ In need of answers
I didn't think about my breakup when I:	☐ Fearful
	☐ Peaceful
	☐ Acceptance
	☐ Forgiveness

The biggest challenge I faced today was:

I experienced a "boss up" moment today when I:

I felt at peace today when I:

I loved myself today when I:

I am: (List three positive attributes about yourself)

1.

2.

3.

I am working to improve myself in these areas:

I'M DOING ME...SELF-REFLECTIONS

Date: /   /

	Today I Feel:
I thought about my ex today and I:	☐ Stressed
	☐ Tearful
I made myself a priority today by:	☐ Angry
	☐ Sad
	☐ Lonely
	☐ In need of answers
I didn't think about my breakup when I:	☐ Fearful
	☐ Peaceful
	☐ Acceptance
	☐ Forgiveness

The biggest challenge I faced today was:

I experienced a "boss up" moment today when I:

I felt at peace today when I:

I loved myself today when I:

I am: (List three positive attributes about yourself)

1.

2.

3.

I am working to improve myself in these areas:

I'M DOING ME...SELF-REFLECTIONS

Date: /   /

I thought about my ex today and I:	**Today I Feel:** ☐ Stressed ☐ Tearful
I made myself a priority today by:	☐ Angry ☐ Sad ☐ Lonely ☐ In need of answers
I didn't think about my breakup when I:	☐ Fearful ☐ Peaceful ☐ Acceptance ☐ Forgiveness

The biggest challenge I faced today was:

I experienced a "boss up" moment today when I:

I felt at peace today when I:

I loved myself today when I:

I am: (List three positive attributes about yourself)

1.

2.

3.

I am working to improve myself in these areas:

I'M DOING ME...SELF-REFLECTIONS

Date: /   /

	Today I Feel:
I thought about my ex today and I:	☐ Stressed ☐ Tearful
I made myself a priority today by:	☐ Angry ☐ Sad ☐ Lonely ☐ In need of answers
I didn't think about my breakup when I:	☐ Fearful ☐ Peaceful ☐ Acceptance ☐ Forgiveness

The biggest challenge I faced today was:

I experienced a "boss up" moment today when I:

I felt at peace today when I:

I loved myself today when I:

I am: (List three positive attributes about yourself)

1.

2.

3.

I am working to improve myself in these areas:

I'M DOING ME...SELF-REFLECTIONS

Date: /   /

I thought about my ex today and I:	**Today I Feel:** ☐ Stressed ☐ Tearful
I made myself a priority today by:	☐ Angry ☐ Sad ☐ Lonely ☐ In need of answers
I didn't think about my breakup when I:	☐ Fearful ☐ Peaceful ☐ Acceptance ☐ Forgiveness

The biggest challenge I faced today was:

I experienced a "boss up" moment today when I:

I felt at peace today when I:

I loved myself today when I:

I am: (List three positive attributes about yourself)

1.

2.

3.

I am working to improve myself in these areas:

I'M DOING ME...SELF-REFLECTIONS

Date: /   /

I thought about my ex today and I:	**Today I Feel:** ☐ Stressed ☐ Tearful
I made myself a priority today by:	☐ Angry ☐ Sad ☐ Lonely ☐ In need of answers
I didn't think about my breakup when I:	☐ Fearful ☐ Peaceful ☐ Acceptance ☐ Forgiveness

The biggest challenge I faced today was:

I experienced a "boss up" moment today when I:

I felt at peace today when I:

I loved myself today when I:

I am: (List three positive attributes about yourself)

1.

2.

3.

I am working to improve myself in these areas:

I'M DOING ME...SELF-REFLECTIONS

Date: /   /

I thought about my ex today and I:	**Today I Feel:** ☐ Stressed ☐ Tearful
I made myself a priority today by:	☐ Angry ☐ Sad ☐ Lonely ☐ In need of answers
I didn't think about my breakup when I:	☐ Fearful ☐ Peaceful ☐ Acceptance ☐ Forgiveness

The biggest challenge I faced today was:

I experienced a "boss up" moment today when I:

I felt at peace today when I:

I loved myself today when I:

I am: (List three positive attributes about yourself)

1.

2.

3.

I am working to improve myself in these areas:

I'M DOING ME...SELF-REFLECTIONS

Date: /   /

	Today I Feel:
I thought about my ex today and I:	☐ Stressed
	☐ Tearful
I made myself a priority today by:	☐ Angry
	☐ Sad
	☐ Lonely
	☐ In need of answers
I didn't think about my breakup when I:	☐ Fearful
	☐ Peaceful
	☐ Acceptance
	☐ Forgiveness

The biggest challenge I faced today was:

I experienced a "boss up" moment today when I:

I felt at peace today when I:

I loved myself today when I:

I am: (List three positive attributes about yourself)

1.

2.

3.

I am working to improve myself in these areas:

I'M DOING ME...SELF-REFLECTIONS

Date: /   /

	Today I Feel:
I thought about my ex today and I:	☐ Stressed
	☐ Tearful
I made myself a priority today by:	☐ Angry
	☐ Sad
	☐ Lonely
	☐ In need of answers
I didn't think about my breakup when I:	☐ Fearful
	☐ Peaceful
	☐ Acceptance
	☐ Forgiveness

The biggest challenge I faced today was:

I experienced a "boss up" moment today when I:

I felt at peace today when I:

I loved myself today when I:

I am: (List three positive attributes about yourself)

1.

2.

3.

I am working to improve myself in these areas:

I'M DOING ME...SELF-REFLECTIONS

Date: /   /

I thought about my ex today and I:	**Today I Feel:**
	☐ Stressed
	☐ Tearful
I made myself a priority today by:	☐ Angry
	☐ Sad
	☐ Lonely
	☐ In need of answers
I didn't think about my breakup when I:	☐ Fearful
	☐ Peaceful
	☐ Acceptance
	☐ Forgiveness

The biggest challenge I faced today was:

I experienced a "boss up" moment today when I:

I felt at peace today when I:

I loved myself today when I:

I am: (List three positive attributes about yourself)

1.

2.

3.

I am working to improve myself in these areas:

I'M DOING ME...SELF-REFLECTIONS

Date: /   /

	Today I Feel:
I thought about my ex today and I:	☐ Stressed ☐ Tearful
I made myself a priority today by:	☐ Angry ☐ Sad ☐ Lonely ☐ In need of answers
I didn't think about my breakup when I:	☐ Fearful ☐ Peaceful ☐ Acceptance ☐ Forgiveness

The biggest challenge I faced today was:

I experienced a "boss up" moment today when I:

I felt at peace today when I:

I loved myself today when I:

I am: (List three positive attributes about yourself)

1.

2.

3.

I am working to improve myself in these areas:

I'M DOING ME...SELF-REFLECTIONS

Date: /   /

I thought about my ex today and I:	**Today I Feel:**
	☐ Stressed
	☐ Tearful
I made myself a priority today by:	☐ Angry
	☐ Sad
	☐ Lonely
	☐ In need of answers
I didn't think about my breakup when I:	☐ Fearful
	☐ Peaceful
	☐ Acceptance
	☐ Forgiveness

The biggest challenge I faced today was:

I experienced a "boss up" moment today when I:

I felt at peace today when I:

I loved myself today when I:

I am: (List three positive attributes about yourself)

1.

2.

3.

I am working to improve myself in these areas:

I'M DOING ME...SELF-REFLECTIONS

Date: /   /

I thought about my ex today and I:	**Today I Feel:** ☐ Stressed ☐ Tearful
I made myself a priority today by:	☐ Angry ☐ Sad ☐ Lonely ☐ In need of answers
I didn't think about my breakup when I:	☐ Fearful ☐ Peaceful ☐ Acceptance ☐ Forgiveness

The biggest challenge I faced today was:

I experienced a "boss up" moment today when I:

I felt at peace today when I:

I loved myself today when I:

I am: (List three positive attributes about yourself)

1.

2.

3.

I am working to improve myself in these areas:

I'M DOING ME...SELF-REFLECTIONS

Date: /   /

	Today I Feel:
I thought about my ex today and I:	☐ Stressed
	☐ Tearful
I made myself a priority today by:	☐ Angry
	☐ Sad
	☐ Lonely
	☐ In need of answers
I didn't think about my breakup when I:	☐ Fearful
	☐ Peaceful
	☐ Acceptance
	☐ Forgiveness

The biggest challenge I faced today was:

I experienced a "boss up" moment today when I:

I felt at peace today when I:

I loved myself today when I:

I am: (List three positive attributes about yourself)

1.

2.

3.

I am working to improve myself in these areas:

I'M DOING ME...SELF-REFLECTIONS

Date: /   /

I thought about my ex today and I:	**Today I Feel:**
	☐ Stressed
	☐ Tearful
I made myself a priority today by:	☐ Angry
	☐ Sad
	☐ Lonely
	☐ In need of answers
I didn't think about my breakup when I:	☐ Fearful
	☐ Peaceful
	☐ Acceptance
	☐ Forgiveness

The biggest challenge I faced today was:

I experienced a "boss up" moment today when I:

I felt at peace today when I:

I loved myself today when I:

I am: (List three positive attributes about yourself)

1.

2.

3.

I am working to improve myself in these areas:

I'M DOING ME...SELF-REFLECTIONS

Date: /   /

I thought about my ex today and I:	**Today I Feel:** ☐ Stressed ☐ Tearful
I made myself a priority today by:	☐ Angry ☐ Sad ☐ Lonely ☐ In need of answers
I didn't think about my breakup when I:	☐ Fearful ☐ Peaceful ☐ Acceptance ☐ Forgiveness

The biggest challenge I faced today was:

I experienced a "boss up" moment today when I:

I felt at peace today when I:

I loved myself today when I:

I am: (List three positive attributes about yourself)

1.

2.

3.

I am working to improve myself in these areas:

I'M DOING ME...SELF-REFLECTIONS

Date: /   /

I thought about my ex today and I:	**Today I Feel:**
	☐ Stressed
	☐ Tearful
I made myself a priority today by:	☐ Angry
	☐ Sad
	☐ Lonely
	☐ In need of answers
I didn't think about my breakup when I:	☐ Fearful
	☐ Peaceful
	☐ Acceptance
	☐ Forgiveness

The biggest challenge I faced today was:

I experienced a "boss up" moment today when I:

I felt at peace today when I:

I loved myself today when I:

I am: (List three positive attributes about yourself)

1.

2.

3.

I am working to improve myself in these areas:

I'M DOING ME...SELF-REFLECTIONS

Date: / /

	Today I Feel:
I thought about my ex today and I:	☐ Stressed
	☐ Tearful
I made myself a priority today by:	☐ Angry
	☐ Sad
	☐ Lonely
	☐ In need of answers
I didn't think about my breakup when I:	☐ Fearful
	☐ Peaceful
	☐ Acceptance
	☐ Forgiveness

The biggest challenge I faced today was:

I experienced a "boss up" moment today when I:

I felt at peace today when I:

I loved myself today when I:

I am: (List three positive attributes about yourself)

1.

2.

3.

I am working to improve myself in these areas:

I'M DOING ME...SELF-REFLECTIONS

Date: /   /

I thought about my ex today and I:	**Today I Feel:** ☐ Stressed ☐ Tearful
I made myself a priority today by:	☐ Angry ☐ Sad ☐ Lonely ☐ In need of answers
I didn't think about my breakup when I:	☐ Fearful ☐ Peaceful ☐ Acceptance ☐ Forgiveness

The biggest challenge I faced today was:

I experienced a "boss up" moment today when I:

I felt at peace today when I:

I loved myself today when I:

I am: (List three positive attributes about yourself)
1.
2.
3.

I am working to improve myself in these areas:

I'M DOING ME...SELF-REFLECTIONS

Date: /   /

I thought about my ex today and I:	**Today I Feel:**
	☐ Stressed
	☐ Tearful
I made myself a priority today by:	☐ Angry
	☐ Sad
	☐ Lonely
	☐ In need of answers
I didn't think about my breakup when I:	☐ Fearful
	☐ Peaceful
	☐ Acceptance
	☐ Forgiveness

The biggest challenge I faced today was:

I experienced a "boss up" moment today when I:

I felt at peace today when I:

I loved myself today when I:

I am: (List three positive attributes about yourself)

1.

2.

3.

I am working to improve myself in these areas:

I'M DOING ME...SELF-REFLECTIONS

Date: /   /

I thought about my ex today and I:	**Today I Feel:** ☐ Stressed ☐ Tearful
I made myself a priority today by:	☐ Angry ☐ Sad ☐ Lonely ☐ In need of answers
I didn't think about my breakup when I:	☐ Fearful ☐ Peaceful ☐ Acceptance ☐ Forgiveness

The biggest challenge I faced today was:

I experienced a "boss up" moment today when I:

I felt at peace today when I:

I loved myself today when I:

I am: (List three positive attributes about yourself)

1.

2.

3.

I am working to improve myself in these areas:

I'M DOING ME...SELF-REFLECTIONS

Date: __ / __ / __

I thought about my ex today and I:	**Today I Feel:**
	☐ Stressed
	☐ Tearful
I made myself a priority today by:	☐ Angry
	☐ Sad
	☐ Lonely
	☐ In need of answers
I didn't think about my breakup when I:	☐ Fearful
	☐ Peaceful
	☐ Acceptance
	☐ Forgiveness

The biggest challenge I faced today was:

I experienced a "boss up" moment today when I:

I felt at peace today when I:

I loved myself today when I:

I am: (List three positive attributes about yourself)

1.

2.

3.

I am working to improve myself in these areas:

I'M DOING ME...SELF-REFLECTIONS

Date: /   /

I thought about my ex today and I:	**Today I Feel:** ☐ Stressed ☐ Tearful
I made myself a priority today by:	☐ Angry ☐ Sad ☐ Lonely ☐ In need of answers
I didn't think about my breakup when I:	☐ Fearful ☐ Peaceful ☐ Acceptance ☐ Forgiveness

The biggest challenge I faced today was:

I experienced a "boss up" moment today when I:

I felt at peace today when I:

I loved myself today when I:

I am: (List three positive attributes about yourself)

1.

2.

3.

I am working to improve myself in these areas:

I'M DOING ME...SELF-REFLECTIONS

Date: / /

I thought about my ex today and I:	**Today I Feel:**
	☐ Stressed
	☐ Tearful
I made myself a priority today by:	☐ Angry
	☐ Sad
	☐ Lonely
	☐ In need of answers
I didn't think about my breakup when I:	☐ Fearful
	☐ Peaceful
	☐ Acceptance
	☐ Forgiveness

The biggest challenge I faced today was:

I experienced a "boss up" moment today when I:

I felt at peace today when I:

I loved myself today when I:

I am: (List three positive attributes about yourself)

1.

2.

3.

I am working to improve myself in these areas:

I'M DOING ME...SELF-REFLECTIONS

Date: /   /

	Today I Feel:
I thought about my ex today and I:	☐ Stressed
	☐ Tearful
I made myself a priority today by:	☐ Angry
	☐ Sad
	☐ Lonely
	☐ In need of answers
I didn't think about my breakup when I:	☐ Fearful
	☐ Peaceful
	☐ Acceptance
	☐ Forgiveness

The biggest challenge I faced today was:

I experienced a "boss up" moment today when I:

I felt at peace today when I:

I loved myself today when I:

I am: (List three positive attributes about yourself)

1.

2.

3.

I am working to improve myself in these areas:

I'M DOING ME...SELF-REFLECTIONS

Date: /   /

I thought about my ex today and I:	Today I Feel:
	☐ Stressed
	☐ Tearful
I made myself a priority today by:	☐ Angry
	☐ Sad
	☐ Lonely
	☐ In need of answers
I didn't think about my breakup when I:	☐ Fearful
	☐ Peaceful
	☐ Acceptance
	☐ Forgiveness

The biggest challenge I faced today was:

I experienced a "boss up" moment today when I:

I felt at peace today when I:

I loved myself today when I:

I am: (List three positive attributes about yourself)

1.

2.

3.

I am working to improve myself in these areas:

I'M DOING ME...SELF-REFLECTIONS

Date: /   /

I thought about my ex today and I:	**Today I Feel:** ☐ Stressed ☐ Tearful
I made myself a priority today by:	☐ Angry ☐ Sad ☐ Lonely ☐ In need of answers
I didn't think about my breakup when I:	☐ Fearful ☐ Peaceful ☐ Acceptance ☐ Forgiveness

The biggest challenge I faced today was:

I experienced a "boss up" moment today when I:

I felt at peace today when I:

I loved myself today when I:

I am: (List three positive attributes about yourself)

1.

2.

3.

I am working to improve myself in these areas:

I'M DOING ME...SELF-REFLECTIONS

Date: /   /

I thought about my ex today and I:	**Today I Feel:**
	☐ Stressed
	☐ Tearful
I made myself a priority today by:	☐ Angry
	☐ Sad
	☐ Lonely
	☐ In need of answers
I didn't think about my breakup when I:	☐ Fearful
	☐ Peaceful
	☐ Acceptance
	☐ Forgiveness

The biggest challenge I faced today was:

I experienced a "boss up" moment today when I:

I felt at peace today when I:

I loved myself today when I:

I am: (List three positive attributes about yourself)

1.

2.

3.

I am working to improve myself in these areas:

I'M DOING ME...SELF-REFLECTIONS

Date: / /

	Today I Feel:
I thought about my ex today and I:	☐ Stressed
	☐ Tearful
I made myself a priority today by:	☐ Angry
	☐ Sad
	☐ Lonely
	☐ In need of answers
I didn't think about my breakup when I:	☐ Fearful
	☐ Peaceful
	☐ Acceptance
	☐ Forgiveness

The biggest challenge I faced today was:

I experienced a "boss up" moment today when I:

I felt at peace today when I:

I loved myself today when I:

I am: (List three positive attributes about yourself)

1.

2.

3.

I am working to improve myself in these areas:

I'M DOING ME...SELF-REFLECTIONS

Date: / /

	Today I Feel:
I thought about my ex today and I:	☐ Stressed
	☐ Tearful
I made myself a priority today by:	☐ Angry
	☐ Sad
	☐ Lonely
	☐ In need of answers
I didn't think about my breakup when I:	☐ Fearful
	☐ Peaceful
	☐ Acceptance
	☐ Forgiveness

The biggest challenge I faced today was:

I experienced a "boss up" moment today when I:

I felt at peace today when I:

I loved myself today when I:

I am: (List three positive attributes about yourself)

1.

2.

3.

I am working to improve myself in these areas:

I'M DOING ME...SELF-REFLECTIONS

Date: /   /

I thought about my ex today and I:	**Today I Feel:** ☐ Stressed ☐ Tearful ☐ Angry ☐ Sad ☐ Lonely ☐ In need of answers ☐ Fearful ☐ Peaceful ☐ Acceptance ☐ Forgiveness
I made myself a priority today by:	
I didn't think about my breakup when I:	

The biggest challenge I faced today was:

I experienced a "boss up" moment today when I:

I felt at peace today when I:

I loved myself today when I:

I am: (List three positive attributes about yourself)

1.

2.

3.

I am working to improve myself in these areas:

I'M DOING ME...SELF-REFLECTIONS

Date: / /

I thought about my ex today and I:	**Today I Feel:**
	☐ Stressed
	☐ Tearful
I made myself a priority today by:	☐ Angry
	☐ Sad
	☐ Lonely
	☐ In need of answers
I didn't think about my breakup when I:	☐ Fearful
	☐ Peaceful
	☐ Acceptance
	☐ Forgiveness

The biggest challenge I faced today was:

I experienced a "boss up" moment today when I:

I felt at peace today when I:

I loved myself today when I:

I am: (List three positive attributes about yourself)

1.

2.

3.

I am working to improve myself in these areas:

I'M DOING ME...SELF-REFLECTIONS

Date: /   /

I thought about my ex today and I:	**Today I Feel:**
	☐ Stressed
	☐ Tearful
I made myself a priority today by:	☐ Angry
	☐ Sad
	☐ Lonely
	☐ In need of answers
I didn't think about my breakup when I:	☐ Fearful
	☐ Peaceful
	☐ Acceptance
	☐ Forgiveness

The biggest challenge I faced today was:

I experienced a "boss up" moment today when I:

I felt at peace today when I:

I loved myself today when I:

I am: (List three positive attributes about yourself)

1.

2.

3.

I am working to improve myself in these areas:

I'M DOING ME...SELF-REFLECTIONS

Date: /   /

I thought about my ex today and I:	**Today I Feel:**
	☐ Stressed
	☐ Tearful
I made myself a priority today by:	☐ Angry
	☐ Sad
	☐ Lonely
	☐ In need of answers
I didn't think about my breakup when I:	☐ Fearful
	☐ Peaceful
	☐ Acceptance
	☐ Forgiveness

The biggest challenge I faced today was:

I experienced a "boss up" moment today when I:

I felt at peace today when I:

I loved myself today when I:

I am: (List three positive attributes about yourself)

1.

2.

3.

I am working to improve myself in these areas:

I'M DOING ME...SELF-REFLECTIONS

Date: /   /

I thought about my ex today and I:	Today I Feel:
	☐ Stressed
	☐ Tearful
I made myself a priority today by:	☐ Angry
	☐ Sad
	☐ Lonely
	☐ In need of answers
I didn't think about my breakup when I:	☐ Fearful
	☐ Peaceful
	☐ Acceptance
	☐ Forgiveness

The biggest challenge I faced today was:

I experienced a "boss up" moment today when I:

I felt at peace today when I:

I loved myself today when I:

I am: (List three positive attributes about yourself)

1.

2.

3.

I am working to improve myself in these areas:

I'M DOING ME...SELF-REFLECTIONS

Date: /   /

I thought about my ex today and I:	Today I Feel:
	☐ Stressed
	☐ Tearful
I made myself a priority today by:	☐ Angry
	☐ Sad
	☐ Lonely
	☐ In need of answers
I didn't think about my breakup when I:	☐ Fearful
	☐ Peaceful
	☐ Acceptance
	☐ Forgiveness

The biggest challenge I faced today was:

I experienced a "boss up" moment today when I:

I felt at peace today when I:

I loved myself today when I:

I am: (List three positive attributes about yourself)

1.

2.

3.

I am working to improve myself in these areas:

I'M DOING ME...SELF-REFLECTIONS

Date: /   /

I thought about my ex today and I:	**Today I Feel:** ☐ Stressed ☐ Tearful
I made myself a priority today by:	☐ Angry ☐ Sad ☐ Lonely ☐ In need of answers
I didn't think about my breakup when I:	☐ Fearful ☐ Peaceful ☐ Acceptance ☐ Forgiveness

The biggest challenge I faced today was:

I experienced a "boss up" moment today when I:

I felt at peace today when I:

I loved myself today when I:

I am: (List three positive attributes about yourself)

1.

2.

3.

I am working to improve myself in these areas:

I'M DOING ME...SELF-REFLECTIONS

Date: /   /

I thought about my ex today and I:	**Today I Feel:** ☐ Stressed ☐ Tearful
I made myself a priority today by:	☐ Angry ☐ Sad ☐ Lonely ☐ In need of answers
I didn't think about my breakup when I:	☐ Fearful ☐ Peaceful ☐ Acceptance ☐ Forgiveness

The biggest challenge I faced today was:

I experienced a "boss up" moment today when I:

I felt at peace today when I:

I loved myself today when I:

I am: (List three positive attributes about yourself)

1.

2.

3.

I am working to improve myself in these areas:

I'M DOING ME...SELF-REFLECTIONS

Date: /   /

I thought about my ex today and I:	**Today I Feel:**
	☐ Stressed
	☐ Tearful
I made myself a priority today by:	☐ Angry
	☐ Sad
	☐ Lonely
	☐ In need of answers
I didn't think about my breakup when I:	☐ Fearful
	☐ Peaceful
	☐ Acceptance
	☐ Forgiveness

The biggest challenge I faced today was:

I experienced a "boss up" moment today when I:

I felt at peace today when I:

I loved myself today when I:

I am: (List three positive attributes about yourself)

1.

2.

3.

I am working to improve myself in these areas:

I'M DOING ME...SELF-REFLECTIONS

Date: /   /

I thought about my ex today and I:	**Today I Feel:** ☐ Stressed ☐ Tearful
I made myself a priority today by:	☐ Angry ☐ Sad ☐ Lonely ☐ In need of answers
I didn't think about my breakup when I:	☐ Fearful ☐ Peaceful ☐ Acceptance ☐ Forgiveness

The biggest challenge I faced today was:

I experienced a "boss up" moment today when I:

I felt at peace today when I:

I loved myself today when I:

I am: (List three positive attributes about yourself)

1.

2.

3.

I am working to improve myself in these areas:

I'M DOING ME...SELF-REFLECTIONS

Date: /   /

I thought about my ex today and I:	**Today I Feel:**
	☐ Stressed
	☐ Tearful
I made myself a priority today by:	☐ Angry
	☐ Sad
	☐ Lonely
	☐ In need of answers
I didn't think about my breakup when I:	☐ Fearful
	☐ Peaceful
	☐ Acceptance
	☐ Forgiveness

The biggest challenge I faced today was:

I experienced a "boss up" moment today when I:

I felt at peace today when I:

I loved myself today when I:

I am: (List three positive attributes about yourself)

1.

2.

3.

I am working to improve myself in these areas:

I'M DOING ME...SELF-REFLECTIONS

Date: /   /

I thought about my ex today and I:	Today I Feel:
	☐ Stressed
	☐ Tearful
I made myself a priority today by:	☐ Angry
	☐ Sad
	☐ Lonely
	☐ In need of answers
I didn't think about my breakup when I:	☐ Fearful
	☐ Peaceful
	☐ Acceptance
	☐ Forgiveness

The biggest challenge I faced today was:

I experienced a "boss up" moment today when I:

I felt at peace today when I:

I loved myself today when I:

I am: (List three positive attributes about yourself)

1.

2.

3.

I am working to improve myself in these areas:

I'M DOING ME...SELF-REFLECTIONS

Date: /   /

	Today I Feel:
I thought about my ex today and I:	☐ Stressed
	☐ Tearful
I made myself a priority today by:	☐ Angry
	☐ Sad
	☐ Lonely
I didn't think about my breakup when I:	☐ In need of answers
	☐ Fearful
	☐ Peaceful
	☐ Acceptance
	☐ Forgiveness

The biggest challenge I faced today was:

I experienced a "boss up" moment today when I:

I felt at peace today when I:

I loved myself today when I:

I am: (List three positive attributes about yourself)

1.

2.

3.

I am working to improve myself in these areas:

I'M DOING ME...SELF-REFLECTIONS

Date: /   /

I thought about my ex today and I:	**Today I Feel:** ☐ Stressed ☐ Tearful
I made myself a priority today by:	☐ Angry ☐ Sad ☐ Lonely
	☐ In need of answers
I didn't think about my breakup when I:	☐ Fearful ☐ Peaceful ☐ Acceptance ☐ Forgiveness

The biggest challenge I faced today was:

I experienced a "boss up" moment today when I:

I felt at peace today when I:

I loved myself today when I:

I am: (List three positive attributes about yourself)

1.

2.

3.

I am working to improve myself in these areas:

I'M DOING ME...SELF-REFLECTIONS

Date: /   /

	Today I Feel:
I thought about my ex today and I:	☐ Stressed
	☐ Tearful
I made myself a priority today by:	☐ Angry
	☐ Sad
	☐ Lonely
	☐ In need of answers
I didn't think about my breakup when I:	☐ Fearful
	☐ Peaceful
	☐ Acceptance
	☐ Forgiveness

The biggest challenge I faced today was:

I experienced a "boss up" moment today when I:

I felt at peace today when I:

I loved myself today when I:

I am: (List three positive attributes about yourself)

1.

2.

3.

I am working to improve myself in these areas:

I'M DOING ME...SELF-REFLECTIONS

Date: /   /

I thought about my ex today and I:	**Today I Feel:**
	☐ Stressed
	☐ Tearful
I made myself a priority today by:	☐ Angry
	☐ Sad
	☐ Lonely
	☐ In need of answers
I didn't think about my breakup when I:	☐ Fearful
	☐ Peaceful
	☐ Acceptance
	☐ Forgiveness

The biggest challenge I faced today was:

I experienced a "boss up" moment today when I:

I felt at peace today when I:

I loved myself today when I:

I am: (List three positive attributes about yourself)

1.

2.

3.

I am working to improve myself in these areas:

I'M DOING ME...SELF-REFLECTIONS

Date: /   /

I thought about my ex today and I:	**Today I Feel:**
	☐ Stressed
	☐ Tearful
I made myself a priority today by:	☐ Angry
	☐ Sad
	☐ Lonely
	☐ In need of answers
I didn't think about my breakup when I:	☐ Fearful
	☐ Peaceful
	☐ Acceptance
	☐ Forgiveness

The biggest challenge I faced today was:

I experienced a "boss up" moment today when I:

I felt at peace today when I:

I loved myself today when I:

I am: (List three positive attributes about yourself)

1.

2.

3.

I am working to improve myself in these areas:

I'M DOING ME...SELF-REFLECTIONS

Date: /   /

	Today I Feel:
I thought about my ex today and I:	☐ Stressed
	☐ Tearful
I made myself a priority today by:	☐ Angry
	☐ Sad
	☐ Lonely
	☐ In need of answers
I didn't think about my breakup when I:	☐ Fearful
	☐ Peaceful
	☐ Acceptance
	☐ Forgiveness

The biggest challenge I faced today was:

I experienced a "boss up" moment today when I:

I felt at peace today when I:

I loved myself today when I:

I am: (List three positive attributes about yourself)

1.

2.

3.

I am working to improve myself in these areas:

I'M DOING ME...SELF-REFLECTIONS

Date: ___ / ___ / ___

	Today I Feel:
I thought about my ex today and I:	☐ Stressed
	☐ Tearful
I made myself a priority today by:	☐ Angry
	☐ Sad
	☐ Lonely
	☐ In need of answers
I didn't think about my breakup when I:	☐ Fearful
	☐ Peaceful
	☐ Acceptance
	☐ Forgiveness

The biggest challenge I faced today was:

I experienced a "boss up" moment today when I:

I felt at peace today when I:

I loved myself today when I:

I am: (List three positive attributes about yourself)

1.

2.

3.

I am working to improve myself in these areas:

I'M DOING ME...SELF-REFLECTIONS

Date: /   /

	Today I Feel:
I thought about my ex today and I:	☐ Stressed ☐ Tearful
I made myself a priority today by:	☐ Angry ☐ Sad ☐ Lonely ☐ In need of answers
I didn't think about my breakup when I:	☐ Fearful ☐ Peaceful ☐ Acceptance ☐ Forgiveness

The biggest challenge I faced today was:

I experienced a "boss up" moment today when I:

I felt at peace today when I:

I loved myself today when I:

I am: (List three positive attributes about yourself)

1.

2.

3.

I am working to improve myself in these areas:

I'M DOING ME...SELF-REFLECTIONS

I thought about my ex today and I:	**Today I Feel:**
	☐ Stressed
	☐ Tearful
I made myself a priority today by:	☐ Angry
	☐ Sad
	☐ Lonely
	☐ In need of answers
I didn't think about my breakup when I:	☐ Fearful
	☐ Peaceful
	☐ Acceptance
	☐ Forgiveness

The biggest challenge I faced today was:

I experienced a "boss up" moment today when I:

I felt at peace today when I:

I loved myself today when I:

I am: (List three positive attributes about yourself)

1.

2.

3.

I am working to improve myself in these areas:

I'M DOING ME...SELF-REFLECTIONS

Date: /   /

I thought about my ex today and I:	**Today I Feel:** ☐ Stressed ☐ Tearful
I made myself a priority today by:	☐ Angry ☐ Sad ☐ Lonely ☐ In need of answers
I didn't think about my breakup when I:	☐ Fearful ☐ Peaceful ☐ Acceptance ☐ Forgiveness

The biggest challenge I faced today was:

I experienced a "boss up" moment today when I:

I felt at peace today when I:

I loved myself today when I:

I am: (List three positive attributes about yourself)

1.

2.

3.

I am working to improve myself in these areas:

I'M DOING ME...SELF-REFLECTIONS

Date: /   /

I thought about my ex today and I:	**Today I Feel:**
	☐ Stressed
	☐ Tearful
I made myself a priority today by:	☐ Angry
	☐ Sad
	☐ Lonely
	☐ In need of answers
I didn't think about my breakup when I:	☐ Fearful
	☐ Peaceful
	☐ Acceptance
	☐ Forgiveness

The biggest challenge I faced today was:

I experienced a "boss up" moment today when I:

I felt at peace today when I:

I loved myself today when I:

I am: (List three positive attributes about yourself)

1.

2.

3.

I am working to improve myself in these areas:

ARE YOU READY TO GET BACK TO "FEELING GOOD AS HELL?"

It's going to take time, energy, and effort to bounce back from the relationship ending. As time goes on and you learn to prioritize, your ex will start to become part of your distant past. You'll begin to notice the little things in life that you once overlooked. You'll see that a bluebird sits on your windowsill every morning or that your neighborhood has a park that you once drove past every day and ignored. If you didn't burn any bridges with your circle of support when you were with your ex, you'd remember why you chose them to be your circle of support. Then, one day, you'll wake up and realize that 24 hours, 1-month, 2-months, and then 6-months have gone by, and you have not even thought about your ex.

That's when Lizzo's song **"Good as Hell"** suddenly becomes your theme song, and it goes a little something like this:

Woo girl, need to kick off your shoes

Got to take a deep breath, time to focus on you

All the big fights, long nights that you been through

I got a bottle of Tequila I been saving for you

Boss up and change your life

You can have it all, no sacrifice

I know he did you wrong, we can make it right

So go and let it all hang out tonight

OTHER GUIDED JOURNALS & DIARIES
—— by ——
KINYATTA E. GRAY

I Miss You...

Daily Writing Prompts for Reflection, Remembrance, and Spirit Renewal

Fashionista's Travel Diary

A Guided Travel Diary for Travel Planning & Reflections

Kinyatta E. Gray is a Best-Selling Author, Travel Influencer and the CEO of FlightsInStilettos, LLC. Kinyatta is also the Chief Beach Towel Designer for the FlightsInStilettos Glam Girl Beach Towels.

Websites:
https://www.flightsinstilettos.com/

https://www.kinyattagray.com/